HE PASSENGER /   NOTES FROM THE PASSENGER /

HE PASSENGER /   NOTES FROM THE PASSENGER /

/ POEMS

/ GILLIAN CONOLEY

NIGHTBOAT BOOKS
NEW YORK

ISBN: 978-1-64362-172-2

COVER ART
William Kentridge
Drawing for "Zeno Writing" (Landscape, text fragments), 2002
Charcoal on paper
31 1/2 x 47 5/8 in. / (80 x121 cm)
Courtesy of the artist
and Marian Goodman Gallery
Copyright: William Kentridge

DESIGN AND TYPESETTING
adam b. bohannon
Typeset in Adobe Caslon

Cataloging-in-publication data is available from the Library of Congress

Nightboat Books
New York
www.nightboat.org

CONTENTS

V.

"the possibility of joy in the face of death"

VI.

"Tell me, how long have we been dead?"

GEORG TRAKL

"Infinite-limited, is it you?"

MAURICE BLANCHOT

I.

The Passenger

Once and for all mind-wanderings of the passenger.

The beer garden's

composure in its death rattle,

   green partitions, scaled walls, backstroking

     waterways, lure to lure—

                 The passenger rejects projection,

                   its limpid, mirror-like distortion—

prefers vibratory qualities of the seat cushion,

   a spreading of the hands.

The passenger walked without destination for years

   without aging, in open sorrow.

          A suitcase out of which everything had fallen by the wayside, bit by bit,

           as though a salesperson without ware.

          Along sidewalks, discarded nurse caps, the gloves of queens, a demolition of the route, in the deep mycorrhizal network

between whitebark pine and subalpine conifers,

the passenger began to step and swerve in an unsteady manner,

a hologram projected up against a hieroglyph,

figure drawings in caves

indeterminate, exact, the sun going red, yellow, red, often never, unearthed.

The passenger finished off the memory drink, with its supernova's hyperrelativistic speck.

Sun still more than 4 billion years old, a glimpse, a glint

into Homeric times, when one could pick up

one's chariot with one hand.

Warmed ocean, open country:

It was most like night, this thing we walked into.

The Messenger

The messenger came without papers and song

out of sleep unharmed

A guide figure at a pitstop

Digestive issues, a tingling sore throat

at all times the time

between technologies dripped

A rain silver-tinged

translucenced into day

Pink blue shade   of one unidentified   flower bush   the messenger

took a sprig couldn't say

       I am a messenger with epistolary anthropological epigenetic trauma

   some deep ancestral thing floats over the greening hills

surely you understand this the messenger said, at a loss—

The messenger had no distinguishing physical characteristics but was more a feeling

       that all was going to be made clear,

necrotic silence in a shed

                              a peaceful death

                              inside a bunker,   an overheated RV

roamed holding screen and air   one could still breathe out of a twizzle stick—

The messenger was part of

the deep urge to sit, stand, lie down

in an aura of intimacy

awaiting the message

the charged surround

data claims we open

around fifteen times a day

awaiting the message it does not matter

what one secretes or imbibes

weather is a serotonin permafrost

a lickable flame

The messenger would sometimes appear stretched out before the monument

overgrown dragonflies iridescent at pears flit mortality over the body picking up pears

the body that is grounded by the planet.

I have sent you a moonstone talisman via snail mail! says the messenger,

attempting friendliness. Also, PAIN IS EVERYWHERE.

WAR NEVER CLEANSES.

In her silk coat pocket

the algorithm fibrillating,

the messenger wanted an implant in the hand the size of a grain of rice

to get shopping done the black-out curtains drawn

under a sun color of fresh salmon now frozen some said

    A new seasoning of smoke and ash

      sprinkled over slices of mango would portend

        the messenger was of temporary noncitizenship

in an exclusive, genderless, paradisiacal future universe, an orb

where we take a car,　—an invaginated spermicide

down pathways to an old

belief system turned glassine

on which on either side we who were awaiting the message in an aura of intimacy

peered, looking through, smitten by the mystery

of one another, as if that were

the message going all koan

with a worn deck

of red cards　a divining rod

Whispering Technology of a battery clock—

I would love to begin to explain the many voices

plugged in, wires dangling a desire for wind storm

starlings sing to hear themselves it is pleasurable! reply the naturalists

I would love to begin to say something to relieve the onslaught of unleashed

voices but it appears I have fallen down a sky blue tube

in the aura of intimacy awaiting the message

between birth and personhood, death's evensong

enters everyone you love, pierces gut,

and everyone forgets very very slowly

pear's flushed russet in trees

a quiver over history's ossuary of banality and greed,

though roadside tumbles a child's silver bucket, handle still on the pail—

why daylilies why thistle why shoes, hats

to carry departed's

death essence

to those of us remaining among the longest living—

We lost the baby.

Though the baby crowned.

When we loved, we were crowned.

The sorrows returned when our crowns' gems, thorns

ruptured into our skulls:

bombs! bombs!
dick pics and bombs!

The live takes of

how to sweep cages of baby shit

back onto ruling class

I would like to message you but the white powdery appropriation of my throat

cuttlefish songbird vapor

in this body is like a body politic

or stringy cloud, everyone a sage

rising on a platform

a rapture massaged into all of the throats

multi-glottal, the collective dream of art

how even in death or in birth

dust motes glint the perineum a celestial orbit—

The messenger presents the body with a very clean blood in the curse

a headful of ouroboros for a wig if all hair falls out

in the middle of no more money

in orgasm we give ourselves over to the briny substance just under the surface of the divine

somewhere in love remains trust

in the melody in the die-off—

in the clear, clear water the messenger is tracking, dataless

where the mysteries are contemplated

in the true ink and felt

future public orphan of the word

sky blue

clear sky blue

How it was no longer only the country that was divided

It was the order and their words   So that when someone said work

We lay down   so that when someone   said art

Memory was our insufficiency   We caught it in our hands   grievous sharp

After 5 or so years   the T-shirt pills   Every day I say   try throwing it away

To teach my daughter   something new Your grandfather's war helmet, I say

your grandmother's high pile of cottony tresses   the opal axis of her hairpin

steel mink of her closed eye   Something new   Who speaks through your mouth

throw it away   do you want it to say Sister Perpetua   or Mother Apocalypse

on your T-shirt   Tumbling out, a word order reveals   a pack of boys

who unzip to sire   the city seepage   I say   if dust's cosmological   camouflage coats us,

we re-route to another street   I mean, who knows, the house   might not even be here

You, however, are my wonder   fatal, prenatal   as water down a leg   I was born after a war

came of age in a war   leave war everywhere   who speaks through your mouth   won't be me

Something very large and open   and waiting waiting   I errand to fill my hole

You scroll and want worlds   the many worlds of wanting worlds   The gentle body of light

enters the car   slow-surfing   the speedbumps   carrying us along   oceanically because I am vanishing   I think   to show you how but not   just now let's not   talk   just now

Return, return, says the body of light   deciding to not decide   which one of us   to call

into gentle body of light's luscious quandary   settling also into the front seat

transmuted inflamed   our faces our voices   If as mother I gave you mortality

if as daughter you gave me immortality's   brief mirror glint   You are reaching

Into screen to play your music   if this is the end   Empty hands of humanity

will not tomorrow   be enough for you? Mortality upon us with its rosy edge

of want   Mortality upon us with a rosy edge of what   So nothing cannot go unsaid

to pass the night in open air   Saint Perpetua   invented the diary in prison

and after requesting water   knew not to ask   for any other favor

but perseverance of the flesh   I'm green and strong   as live oak   on dry gold grass

I'm blue with externalizing my interior enemies when they are gone I aspirate in primeval mist

James Joyce wrote The Dead   until the last page was snow full

If there is fire   we will pick it up   play with it

Gentle body of light,   I am lonesome pine for you

Who speaks   waits under   the blind glare of Jane Eyre's   mysterious red room

Unlock   and we rivercane   the lyric   you know that patois?

Gentle body of light   you've got such a cruel Ideal

Grievous sharp-nailed coyote   steps at seafoam's edge

If we isolate the isotope   may it rain   in the echo chamber

Gentle body of light, when we're within you   we're outside you   we swim the plasma

We woodshred   the threshold   find airport   by matchlight

Bodies I lie down with in bright grass

Everything a lot

      easier once

I began speaking directly   to the dead

in the crisp air   in the space flying toward me

an invitation   to run to and with

The American Eagle can push a goat off the side of a cliff.   It has no predators.

One she I spotted   OD'd or plagued,   one she   who wished for something a little more

      chthonic than the bald eagle   for our national bird.

Faces sharp as other, steady on.

        Acid-head boyfriends in Vietnam

polyvalent colonialist cinematic warriors on constant replay

My father's WWII scar   across his back diagonally rotted between shoulders,

     a Christian love he walked and talked   and US   took at 22 replaced with a strong scotch in one hand

          a Winston in the other   and more church, church, church

a pew we practically wore through sitting with him.

Why he sang so loud. The in between. An I am other. A why we run. A Paradise–

White Spruce

If all experience

is mystical

the white spruce

swayed in the window

branch by branch almost to the doorstep

willow-like

near your sun-damaged eyes

And what do dirt's

sinuous motions

have to do

with leaf's actions

I asked the young woman

I asked the grandmother

and the entire family

crawling across the floor

And who is the young returnee who

would carry his AK 47 past the 7-11

almost to the corner and back

wanting chips sometimes candy

a contemplative on duty

This wake, sleep, this wake sleep sea

the planet

and its lost parts

lay plow to the furrow

dream a little dream

with me

The Blue Hand

paradise burning again

repetitive in the distillate

marine layer moist under smoke—

a seafoam fiberoptics—

breeze isn't

it was before

or after our deaths

the workplace hipster turned despot

was berating you digitally

since he'd never have to see you again

because covid

because you were getting so old

spittle formed a stalagmite on your lips

both faces and their utterances

were compiled, exchanged,

mistaken for one another

in an inner biomass stew

what got served in prison

on the third day of clear air

a ruby-throated hummingbird

as the neighborhood defamiliarizes

clouds return to break into hawk shadow,   Venmo

wants the instructor,

as the money goes into immaterial

sky you can send money to your friends, she says

just before you wave to friends

if you want to talk hold up the blue hand

it was the new era's fallen window shade crimping dust

time messed up

why nothing felt finished

or even wanted to

the door was too hot to the touch—that's how

you know there was a fire Eurydice

kept turning back to the no one there

in every room paint colors begged

to be reborn The Grey Chalk, The Dark Come Night,

The Puritan Opacity—

a story breaks virally, fungally

on the fifth day the grasshopper

came into the house

the dragonfly, too

with its heavily lidded eyes of extraordinary peripheral vision

we began to climb into

what is the word?

radiation

off the phone a manic glory

as you searched we began to climb into

the data, bank, dinner, amphetamines, jade, turquoise,

equipoise, convexities laced with porosity, air

a "go bag" near window's possible passageway

under the one the hundred thousand

dissimulating lights

by stars the axis unfixed—6 days, 7

do we rest, we wanted to know

are creeks or old nations at least

partially in back of us

what is it with America and division

I have a woman's cramped gut

birthing or not

looking down the barrel of your haze

do you love hate

do you remember solitary

when something barely holds together—

is it divinity—

earth a dirt clod long hot road

that takes us—

river rocks in our pockets—

ever back—

all you ever did,

do you not—

II.

how to have a future memory

how to have a future memory

I will desalinate in cinema if I look long enough and far

from the screen, to the side

to accept all that is

forwarded by mail   to me   in sun   I will

not get ready to die   I shall be   a know-not

in dialect   and coverlet

                              I will turn my mattress over

                              on this voyage

                              leave my guidebook behind

I will kiss in extended swaths of pathogen   I will have will, pact, capture

A quince-colored half-lie, the heart seeks lift

the ear loves conch   dislikes suture

The starlings who mate in space

spray-painted data charts of death rates

climb the underside of the overpass

Beneath blood clot sun

the corpse burned   newborn buckled, strolled   a breeze is made

but can we

trust it

as in if ever you were my lover   if you betrayed me

I hated you hated you hated you   called recalled   you

then heard

a finitude of gladsong

Metal to the skyfull

the plane arrives   waits

and down drop   empty stairs   a white pebble on the tarmac   Where

Have All The People Gone, I will think

                               and grant that I may see you   that you may see me

                               that I am you and we do   that

                               chloroplasts and flagella dust

                               our metatarsal-knitted feet

point   arch   misstep
into two-step   the vanishing

folkdance

                    recalled by deities   who collaborate

under clouds

                Washed to shore could we

step out of our winding cloths

                    sit in folding chairs   where we have made

                                a place   to stay awhile   and watch

our immortalists—our cameras,   our cinema—

the long pleasing ocean shot of sunset   that keeps pulling at our bodies

hotel sheers over the window that billow into body—

over we who do

time in the body—   who climb,

and fall   and fall   and fall

all the dead arrive in skeins

all the dead arrive in skeins, from slopes—out of forests begat in forests—
neglected fields   completely wide out in the open—

in the kitchen.
bodies reeling, unreeled,
                a film. blue.

                        how do   the infected dead
feel about the natural dead
                —and the murdered
dead—no time for that—

        —that
was the living   dodging one another,

folding in upon their families,
        a soft meringue.   berry-stained hands/bone marrow/a faded
                        photo imaging—

the people walk/run/walk, the smell of bread
                a humidity   in which the hair dampens—

decomposition in a body bag—
                        the city's gold day
                        a dispensing chemist.

mucus, fog, mist in the sunny pantry.   psalm/asylum/amaryllis/
                                in dreams, I sweep
                                your forehead, a lavender post-it

each day, morning, noon's rage light—angles down corridors of walking—passes
night—makes such lovely maze, the sun looks back
to dawn—sees who's up—I find you—the feet plant—

the head falls low,
lower, the spine lengthens

A metropole that unpeoples and peoples

The burnt tropic   masticating its vine stock   wand and wind—

Cracked I-phone glass : raying thought, chatter : susurration and aftershock

hair matted   below our ears receiving signals // not all that   synthesizable—

rhythm and phoneme   saying hey there,   hey there

    [until more gessoed grew   the honeydark summer street—

  when you]   coming back—

        sang—

            the heat   —fecund— nightfallen

Partial to sky—tadpoles gone celestial—

Our vocabulary split

into two columns in which : a lexicon likes beginning   —carrion, nightingale—

cloud bank and snow—   A waitress slept in her car for the heat

breathing in   the half-inch of the window   left open

Three Red Plastic Cups

Three red plastic cups point away from
each other, discard
of last night, you read
the signs

the sidewalk has a glow to it

as you get out of your
monstrous car

you rule
the world.

Export, commingle
say when.

Call the shot
of rocket life, Mr. Fireworks'

shuttered stand
The day's one and only contrail

peaks, sky spreads
Once our bodies had more outlets

of affection, those were
days

the ridiculous colors that hung in our closets

rotated,
sort of like crops

to keep the soil
active

A red cup for descent
Two more for ascension   you think

you can understand?
A parking space

reserved for you
knelt down.

III.

Saint Perpetua

Perpetua's diary

We were left no original   papyrus, vellum   no parchment.

Though a redactor soon after 203 CE, date of her martyrdom,

is certain: "she wrote in her own hand and from her own experience."

                                        Felicitas—

    Perpetua's Egyptian slave servant/rumored lover—they are both described

in prison with disheveled hair as though

                let loose like Latin's subordinate clauses—

"I was languishing because I had seen languishing" was one of Perpetua's phrases

                                        ferrying us through time—

Soon before she receives a vision.

"A golden ladder of marvelous light"

"Very narrow" only one person at a time could ascend

each side fixed

" with swords, lances, hooks, daggers"

so if one slipped

one's flesh "would cleave to the iron"

Her brother—among other catechumens—pagans converted to Christianity but not yet

baptized— was first to climb.

He called back down, come, Perpetua, but watch for the dragon's bite.

So she calls on God (who she has come to trust) for help, and slowly, not to scare—
the dragon lifts his head

to serve as the lowest rung on the ladder
on which she steadies her first step

"I trod upon his head"

To garden of "immense extent"

And four angels who lift with no touch

A white haired "shepherd of a large stature

who gave me cheese as it were a little cake"

"I received it with folded hands

and understood that it was to be a passion, not an escape,

and ceased to have any hope in this world."

I don't want to read further because we know the rest of the words aren't hers but a shadow language (redactor left to complete the tale):

      "Walking into

      the arena of wild beasts who had felled Felicitas,

      Perpetua in such state of trance does not feel her own goring and says 'I cannot

tell when we are to be led to that cow'

though sees the gladiator sent to finish the beast's job and places his young wavering hand

and sword

with her own hand to her own throat."

In 1928 a new typeface

By English sculptor and stonemason Eric Gill is given the name Perpetua.

In 2021 Italy   a thin pencil   80% graphite powder derived

from industrial scraps and electrode manufacturing waste

that would otherwise end up in landfill

is also named Perpetua.

"The only pencil in the world able to conduct electricity," says the ad copy.

All ladders columns of light—   or tubes of the possible—

We who were left no original—   gather our resources—

our tools

inks

solvents

resins

pigments

dyes

lubricants

dextrine

glycerine

fluorescents

sediments

think to remain

graphic

recorded

unredacted

alive or dead

or somewhere along the bardic

vast night

and head down foot-first

along the subatomic

nanos in cosmos

best to step carefully among the narrow hydroponic seedlings, recalibrate

just what year it is

when we become uninfectuous though diseased, uncured

like olive trees hundreds of years ago.

Could Perpetua have remained in a state of suspension

cottoning on to a kind of life

frequent with vision—

One further rung

one further loop

quotidian is the diary

"we understood it was to be a passion."

Collective yet separate running

amid wild grasses in our pleasantly disrupted workflow

along blued waters welcoming all sorts of bacteria back and lovingly attached.

And given more time more cells what next would we render

who would be our gods were it not the end but the octave

IV.

When Lie Goes Live

The wind in the trees shuffle a sonic ephemera
under which to feel stable

An hour spent half-seeing stone soldiers in the plaza

In other centuries was it harder to tell
         perception from paranoia
                            dissociation?

         One false fall yellows the leaves all the way to the parking lot

Cheekbones rent a helmet, an odd bend to a branch

         Summer's last tiger lilies deepen, I dreamed my husband

went to war last night, he would never

dream that of me

The actuality of our malfunctioning
disharmonies, steadily,

slowly the papier mache statue of liberty

gets wheeled out to the baseball field
            for the star-spangled, and falls
                        sidelong, and we laugh

but affectionately. I like a man
leaning into white stucco
smoking his pack's last cigarette

                        unknown to the drone,

            the surveillance camera's turned back on itself

an installation site-specific, the soft focus of his eyes
            turning to me while I hang on

to my near empty notebook's low wide white noise

Most streets I sense a solid escape another death

a rupture along each page's glue

                        Pieces of what people say

                                    get repeated internationally

If they catch on long enough
        above the people

                sitting disinterestedly
                mute in a park

The man who went to war
going AWOL by the alarm clock
a pork stew in the
slow cooker

        ham hock for the feds
        who wouldn't know
        what to do with a ham hock, shake or consume

so tired of talking now
though I can't begin

I don't know how I could feed you

I loved, I voted

A holy spirit headache in the rearview
    of the rec center

                    I had a deep no engagement with it
a fatigued member of the populace

        Slow motility in the unharvestable sea
the grain-giving earth

This hand with no war strength in it
            this other that tore perforated rims

    I am a spirit of the come, king, with your comeback face,
    Humor me, queen, I am a have-not have

I am a spirit of other lowly ones for whom your likeness is done

    In the sleek ebb of an old epoch
unseasonably hot amid goose scat

                in the playground where no children were playing
my feet fell out of orbit

    Microphones dangled   inside the eucalyptus   each recorded me

in its hollowed bark

I climbed long civic stairs   no message   no passage

smelling the smell of marigolds like the dead I love

fully assembled in the sun spot

The White House

The house was no longer a toy.

It was beginning to take to the horizon.

It was attaining a righteousness.

It was getting into a facelessness.

Someone tried posting a video of it, a blur

Under a wolf moon, a verdant expanse,

But was shoved down before pressing Send.

We shall have these truths.

Few ever really got to live there.

It was smaller than anyone ever expected.

Its lights were dimmed, though guards remained

In dreamy wigs, roasting pigs, as portraiture

was encouraged in this icebox—

Snow globe, raindrop,

a tiny, naked agent circling the perimeter

as stars appear, disappear in dark skies.

Few acts are intolerable to a house.

Bed mites on night duty.

Riot gear,

A kiln of x=y.

A woman looking up under a glass pane.

A man climbing a wall.

We people, who cease to be useful.

In the next night

In agitation along sleep's surface

dreams the monster, the angular, the slimy, the anything goes, the corpse

who strokes the tigers with rather weak jaws

in a jump cut, on an icy blue couch, red queen

on mute—

                    the nearly taken, the just-about-to-escape voices caught mid-stream

                              say they do not want the story to end when what they mean is

                                        how do we separate

                                        the next night from its screwed-in

light, the weariness of fearing a man in the dark comes a blade out of nowhere

while visionaries we carry like pepper spray

play hangman, visit solitaire,

clear clouds off the moon

so we can see our lady weep, our boy—

genitalia gently shaped into other genitalia

the brain fluid in its cave   each to their own needs

and the old wandering in black robes, opossums, the star magnolia

stilling, trembling, coyotes, foxes,

rats, red and blue states commingled into a silvery waxy balm

with ochre highlights and peach

undertones, a cosmogony

grown distant, unconstituted,

darkness materializing

until every house—if there is a house—

becomes more a faint shed in an interplanetary dust, apothecary-like, something it

would take

a fluoroscope to see—

And the women weep because they have been violated

and not for the first time, and the men clench through what they have done

and the men who did not do it and did not not do it

learn to stand next to the women

a shoulder to shoulder thing   and the women and the men

who had been violated get so exhausted they lie down to spoon

with all who have been violated   the women who did it

The softest of sheets fall

A clef of music occurs

Images (almond soap, tea tree oil) tossed like

wash on wash, clean laundry on top of dirty.

Fascism, facial, fascism, facial,

requiring all the oxygen would inevitably become an elegiac outcome for the human.

Storying all night and dead asleep all day Scheherazade said she did not want to finish when what she meant was

stay, I am a spirit just coffining up his dream timer.

Day done, we sweep

our clippings from a desk.   no end.

near to God, a finish of the finish on a finish in the balm.

In the great chain of unbroken events, story begetting story,

nothing—one voice beside another. at days end, an unclasped necklace

tossed across the dresser, how a pulling at one end makes a slight movement

on the other.

I am only a howl of wind,

no one to make afraid, stay.

In the Next Next World

Day one of the garden I start to get the ground a little wet

before replanting the hacienda creeper

Along earth's curve,

the violet orange sky means it's a save the air day

The she-wolves sprawl on the yard

done dusting the tree trunks with their hides

      —go snake go snake a child yells as she roller skates—

A noon stillness, oxygen or the lack thereof

lacerates on a cellular level

the chemical taste beneath one's beloved's eyes

echoic, piquant, scrubbing out the refrigerator until there is nothing the human propensity to discover and rediscover what was discovered

wet market wayward went the boat

Above my sapien sluggery flew a blue jay all alone

It's growing our own food that makes us revolutionary

the human propensity to discover and rediscover

what was discovered

but how we brace for news and get on with the day is a whole art

the heart breaks and then it mends but you have to thirst for it

as you do for love's work boots

A steep and rocky trail and at its top a muscular arm

one singular limb that has come for you

not to push you but to pull you up and over

as in to haul—

tendons taut tiny strands of fibrils

fingers spread, it is up there on the mountaintop

you may not elide

you may not go home alone

 [you try not to go home alone]

even if you think no one's left but sphere

there is someone [an interlocked

one who waits instead of you]

the acid reflux of your ancestors

a nexus to the morning

a newscast in the evening

the vomiting, you could just hate it, encrypt it

or opiate it, tithe, or kitchen scrap it

I feel a tenant in the barely daylight

I feel a tenant in the barely daylight

A dawn owl in crook of black walnut

Later hail soothed me from the inside

The market felt a portage near the pork barrel

Glaciologist Mariuz Potocki who wasn't allowed to the top of the summit

filled, midway, a small stainless steel jar with snow

to count microplastics' thin, curly fibers

on Mount Everest

Berries in the moors   Some dead friends wish to remain anonymous

Some have little plastic in them   a pelt, a surf, a soft lingering breath

After nightmares'   static-shot   discordant musicals of the bedsheets

I wake to find I am stuffed with cold pragmatics and sweet basil

Under a kindly cloudy sky

I am a video

allowed projection

I say ylang ylang of the custard apple family

yarrow's thin tall yellow green soft spears

historically used for blood clotting

and sticky monkey flower

whose leaves help retain moisture

End Notes

accompaniment   allegro andante

My daughter walks down the hall, says

pretty music,

the potting soil in the car,

why don't you get it out?

Foggy bodhisattva pall of silence in the neighborhood   one towhee   one red-breasted robin.

Oppressive, though a delicate melody.

The corpses, the equations, the creek beneath the lawn

a freshet and a desolation.

rondo   rallentando   recitative

My daughter and I are in a series of animated postures

Martha Graham's with masks as we ready to go out.

Our palms curve up into the room tone.

None of this is eternal.

We make the no dying signal.

We pat our pockets. We have everything.

The day's necrology.

Our hair is falling.

The atmospheric river. Saturn, Jupiter cross.

V.

"the possibility of joy in the face of death"

GEORGES BATAILLE

"the possibility of joy in the face of death"

I.

Couldn't get

"I" nor "we" to settle down, stay unresolved in time   in crisp white burial shirts

              could do   bouts of   theatrical weeping

weary though exacting   avant garde gestures   of the carpenter ant (stoop-start-stop-dive)

before they go underground to breathe

              miracle teachings,   storm drain

                     of the bye, bye, now, honey,

                                          whispery   slow part

of the blues song

              to sour our morals

in the grey oyster wet of the rain

                     weather's excavation   of a childhood doll,   hello beautiful hello so many windows   in the side of a grave   and then an unveiling

of an absolute shadow side, storm drain's   fungal spore

glow worms   neon green   face up   in expanding gasses

in small voids   between soil's   particles

before emerging from their cocoons   as fully adult gnats

                    flying off   to circle
                                          to feed
                                          to pollinate

how to play it

the grave   kind of a farm   waiting there   in the shape of a strung-out guitar

                    how to string it, sling it—

walk away with the family now

    earth seething at our shoes

to make something else of us

around   underneath   our reach—

hello honed, fawn-bone punctum

"the possibility of joy in the face of death"

II.

        what the empty pocketbook's   aura intoned

night's sorcery   lined in a crushed blue red velvet

       color of blood   coursing under skin

     if I thrift   an old pocketbook do I carry   another's DNA

was it she   the "previous owner"   in the compact's mirror her face

     in the residue of powder   who looked back at me

     who had no illusions with immortality

she who was short of a tempest and a moan   had a shrike's tomial tooth

    to help tear prey   leave to thorn   for later

         and when it rained

                 we saw in slant

     a gleaming white shirt   slice through sky

        interpolated   with the season's last hanging walnuts   in their green shells we beneath the rhythm   of roof's calypso ran

it was as if when we spoke   our lips were kissed raw   our throats closed, crowed

"Like you in frames of film arriving in present tense"

"I can trace the way back to my era's hotel—   I still have the desk key"

said the person who tried to speak   for me, she   who would string all this

together she who   would free the rain   from its lyric contract

why do   the living want to wear the dead's   clothes

                    in the familiar limitlessness of a season's glance

I threw away her receipts   each folded tissue   the tag   I knew

            to remain   suspicious of the archive

its slight bleach scent   moldy antihistamine

        its atmospherics of farewells,   carefully wrought invitations

to vanish   "I" would not be a trustee

"the possibility of joy in the face of death"

III.

where one ends and world begins

arrives accident, time slows   a chance to

see what comes to us   or from us

each second's tiny replica

sparks from one's hairbrush

cosmos is guesswork

contemplatives wait in a car

in an air

no longer familiar

or safe to meddle with

the crow can leave gifts for people they like

and have thoughts about their thoughts   this is the sun

"The possibility of joy in the face of death"

IV

Everything as if there shook no fear in the foliage

    At leaves' soft-curled
edges of no fear in
      the foliage

           is
           as if an instruction

within a bardo:

           follow what's left of your clothes

                        Plus, the image had already moved

                        beyond where I had positioned it

Shiny crow feet sidelong on

rooftops of polyhedrons

one rickety carriage of black water

and on the roadside: oxide scattered crystal

Police riot shields held high

when there is all this intermittent shade

       over areas where we have dragged our heels through the dirt

       Black taxis in blue light spasm   a fascism

          in those apps on your phone   stash it

       you little addict

  our collective pubis extraordinaire

      on weekend's night   a soft scarf protects your neurons

I balance the lexicons

as though entering

beaded curtains'

slender voids

or willows' canopies'

willingness to part and contract

to stand in the tiny openings freed

is the sensation an easier version of being born

if you know how to wait

for the human

for the curator, historiographer, and observer

for whom, for whose sake

we want to flower

VI.

Thank You for the Afterlight

for God

the yellow tinged with cyan   primal coat

    the gingerale,   a mother/father figure at first   all face

      the existence that is   a continuance

and extinction, a malted or smoothie

    of the brain freeze, long spinal stretch, and ice age of knowing you, Creator

rile and denial   of the human animal

    buzz saw and honeybee of our correspondence

I reacted to

not unregretfully,   it was

            carried back

       unsigned   I am

writing you   no more

often lies run

a little backwards

 in this missive oblivion

where synapse thinks it saw a spirit

equators shiver

across to one another

     golden tanager and cock-of-the-block

roareth   in the revolution

   on the earth's surface   I know

moment to moment   half

to one third of all thought

is cat vomit really in the middle of the night

  while it was supposed to be medicinal

to eat the grass   this bristly

prelapsarian keyhole of a hut where my finger

lingers   as you   row by

  is that all

to perception   You are like

privileged Ivy League

assessing me   I am

another

white thing

    that little eggshell still stuck on my blouse

I cracked out of you I see that now

  in this skirt rose-splashed, bereft of aura

I love my tiny part Neanderthal DNA

  left, cast-off I go bootless into lyric structures

dump's clear containers

There may have been someone who loved you

more than you loved saving

    that's how you got on this road

and so disfigured

  in land, in word

  standing like a crucifix on a porch while the cars go by

Where   to put   last century's   threadbare Sunday   dress with arms uplift

and begin   to strut a bit

between star and tar

    Celestial nest, also like stress, hormone, breathing with high peaks

        your combustible planetarium,

  an interstitial musculature where

ceiling angels peel and flake a weather

turned glassy in which you

  are the shaken narrator   bundled up

taking a few trips   around the block, running one loose hand over

   the increasingly familiar hedges

     for what have you done

  that so many   run to surround and warm

you, a boy and girl so porous with the air,

   lunar, earthly, I try very hard to never close the parenthesis on you,

  it's one way to atone

   for perhaps you are just swimming

slowly   to another scribe waiting

   sort of perpendicularly   in the lake   near the shore

maybe that's what

    time is

under shaded oak tree's   co-substantiates

the numbers of the house   we come to find

all the while realism's steady message—

someone really loves someone   and then doesn't—

someone almost reads a name

your sinister math   these fits and starts get chalked

then smudged away

into grey otherworldly cloud

on sidewalk's cracked bodice

despite great gusts of pressure

Planet Nexii

Yours ever, fair Star—what do you think

                 that so many of us were partially famous

       at least to ourselves in certain conditions

Some had accrued great comfort, or little,

       or lived in poverty

But we could all touch   could whisper in each other's ears, laugh   and spew, serenade

We were small godlings   if to be a godling   means to be however briefly   available

       walking around with   our weak connections   and melted cords

"People disappear all the time," said one

"Every time they leave the room," said another

in the Antonioni film

No time for divisions said no one, to nowhere,   (the script must have had

a ghost passage)—

"extremely long takes, striking modern architecture, painterly use of color,

tiny human figures adrift in empty landscapes"

(like poetry Antonioni did poorly at the box office)

And the steamy sense of offset characters

plunging their hands into the stewpot

who never met

such a fire as their fire—

I love his convertibles

appearing as if suddenly within your bloodstream how they invite you

to reorient, stand up backwards

fling your arms in air

so alive you feel worthy of being spit on

                    by tree's dew   by one's own back-flown breath

Composed of eons of dissimilation of dead warriors' collective ectoplasm

a cloud swell passed overhead

No matter where one lifts and tilts the globe, battle

and the pulpy colorful raised textures with squiggly black borders

to indicate land. No   nyet   Ne   net. Planet Nexii.

A blue/gray jay,   a cracked, carnelian-colored riverbed   two lovers walk,

returned to thank   Archilochus for the swift the coltish iambic.

The heart a bivalved organ an abundance of muscle designed to one day grow lax, futile

And yet such a strong pulse pours into the ventricle.

Systole, diastole.

The clouds

Notes

"Perpetua's Diary": Saint Perpetua invented the diary in 203 CE in a Roman prison in Carthage while awaiting execution. Her writings are considered one of the earliest Christian texts. The diary is believed to have been edited and redacted by her contemporary Tertullian who claims to have been an eyewitness to her martyrdom, though there remains no definitive scholarly evidence.

"the possibility of joy in the face of death" is Georges Bataille.

The Antonioni film in "Planet Nexii" is *The Passenger*.

"extremely long takes, striking modern architecture, painterly use of color, tiny human figures adrift in empty landscapes" is Stephen Dalton of the British Film Institute.

"Yours Ever, fair star" is John Keats' closing salutation in a letter to Fanny Brawne, July 27, 1819.

Acknowledgements

Thank you to the editors of the magazines where these poems first appeared. Much gratitude and appreciation for your support of the work:

Elizabeth Scanlon, *American Poetry Review*; Brett Fletcher Lauer, *A Public Space*; Garrett Caples, Micah Ballard, and Sunnylyn Thibodeaux, *Castle Grey Skull*; Bradford Morrow, *Conjunctions*; Lucía Hinojosa Gaxiola and Diego Gerard Morrison, *diSONARE*; Emily Wallis Hughes, Jason Zuzga, Rebecca Wolff, *Fence*; Caryl Pagel, Dara Barrois/Dixon and Emily Pettit, *jubilat*; Garrett Caples, Micah Ballard, *High Noon*; and Joshua Marie Wilkinson, *The Volta*.

Enormous thanks and gratitude to Kazim Ali and Julie Carr for generous and thorough readings of the book in manuscript. And to Domenic Stansberry for every single thing, for all the years of conversation, support and light, and to Gillis Stansberry, originary source of grace and love, all that turns and returns.

Most especially, thank you for the inspired integrity and tireless commitment of Stephen Motika, Kazim Ali, Lindsey Boldt, Caelan Ernest Nardone, Gia Gonzales, Lina Bergamini, Jaye Elizabeth Elijah, adam b. bohannon, and all the staff at Nightboat, who steer so much ahead.

GILLIAN CONOLEY is a poet, editor, and translator. The author of ten collections of poetry, Conoley received the Shelley Memorial Award from the Poetry Society of America, and was awarded the Jerome J. Shestack Poetry Prize, a National Endowment for the Arts grant, and a Fund for Poetry Award. *A Little More Red Sun on the Human: New & Selected Poems*, published by Nightboat Books in 2019, won the 39th annual Northern California Award. Conoley's translation of three books by Henri Michaux, *Thousand Times Broken*, appearing in English for the first time, was published in 2014. Conoley has taught at the University of Iowa Writers' Workshop, the University of Denver, Vermont College, and Tulane University. A long-time resident of the San Francisco Bay Area, Conoley is Professor of English and Poet-in-Residence at Sonoma State University. Founder and editor of *Volt* magazine, Conoley has collaborated with installation artist Jenny Holzer, composer Jamie Leigh Sampson, and Butoh dancer Judith Kajuwara.

NIGHTBOAT BOOKS

Nightboat Books, a nonprofit organization, seeks to develop audiences for writers whose work resists convention and transcends boundaries. We publish books rich with poignancy, intelligence, and risk. Please visit nightboat.org to learn about our titles and how you can support our future publications.

The following individuals have supported the publication of this book. We thank them for their generosity and commitment to the mission of Nightboat Books:

Anonymous (4)
Kazim Ali
Abraham Avnisan
Jean C. Ballantyne
The Robert C. Brooks Revocable Trust
Amanda Greenberger
Rachel Lithgow
Anne Marie Macari
Elizabeth Madans
Elizabeth Motika
Thomas Shardlow
Benjamin Taylor
Jerrie Whitfield & Richard Motika

This book is made possible by support from the Topanga Fund, which is dedicated to promoting the arts and literature of California.

In addition, this book is made possible, in part, by grants from the New York City Department of Cultural Affairs in partnership with the City Council and the New York State Council on the Arts Literature Program.